CINDERS

POEMS BY
OWEN D HILL

Author Bio:

I don't like to write about myself, as I feel it places me in a cage that I must break from. A renegade spirit of sorts. A man of many paths, twists and turns along tributaries less traveled. In some cases, traveling while never leaving my seat. My writing is a simple gaze into the beyond inside my mind, as I deal with the mundane daily rituals, we all face.

Blue collar man of many lives, born a hardscrabble son of a convict. Single mother doing what she could. My southern playground was amongst bikers, ne'er-do-wells, and racists. Salt of the earth people with some ugly truths. Where I learned to navigate my own path to seek truth and understanding.

Born in Florida and taken anywhere food stamps were accepted. And many thanks to Toys for Tots for giving me a glimpse of childhood.

In truth under my skin is a tower of cinders, a black and craggy scar laden soul. My hope is that these books make you think about life or about the lives of others and their struggles.

Thank you for choosing to read my words, it means more than I could ever express. Connect with me @owendhill on social or at www.owendhill.com

Also available on Amazon.com:

Be kind Be safe Be human :POEMS

Printed in the United States of America

First Printing, 2020

ISBN 9781661497064

www.owendhill.com or @owendhill

Las Vegas, Nevada

10 9 8 7 6 5 4 3 2 1

CONTENTS

INTRODUCTION

To Whom It May Concern:

Reading through these poems I hope to wrap a layer of mental grime on you, like sticky ashes not easily wiped off. A grime that makes you think about the paths you have not taken but others walk every day. Lives made and destroyed by different decisions in different situations, and against different odds...but intrinsically altogether human.

As a self-reflection in chaos, CINDERS is a perspective on the shared human existence. A context of personal moments as I observe unity in the complex aggregate of life.

My hope is that these words bring forth simultaneously a biting critique of your own views on culture and class while combining an enduring insight that we all can change for the better.

It is a collection of poems as moments in beauty and pain. No heartbreaks, only learning, connection, love, failure, and growth. Exploring these worlds with form and nuance.

...as the world is not a tower of CINDERS and any light that smolders should not scare us.

Respectfully,

Owen D Hill

PLEASE PROMISE A LIE

write me into the future

even if I don't live

through descendants of this vantage

is a page bested read

in the boardgame to create

we find utility

in iron

or irony

OPEN

let your soul breath in the wind

therein lies the song as sang together

never seeing each other again

swayed and changed as is the weather

I want to leave it in

some serendipitous location

as it may find its way into the clutch

of an unsuspecting soul

that needs to hear it

WHICH IS WHAT I NEED

we sit in limbo and I am broke down

I get up standing tall again

to walk this path that we began

love seems to have no place with me

life's beginnings and possibilities

that bring a peace of mind

not a peace that is kind

just simply an answer

which is all I really need

the blind to the blind

pulpit preaching in the blind

music to our ears we fall inline

RELIGIOUS DEATH

if whenever takes me

may it be this side of heaven

although I am not a believer

the chance is left unread

and the man gripping the lever

might be in my head

but if I live life

clean and free

may it keep me

from any dread

MURDER MATRIMONY

police called it murder

in the first degree

I called it justice

for you cheating on me

when I plunged my knife

it was justice

for those tears

they wanted to give me life

but I could only be free

we got that old school kind of love

only death from us do depart

from the knife deep in her heart

even though I am in prison

this ain't no chain on me

FAMILY DEMENTIA

old sore bones got some age on them

an awarded pass to go on ahead

to the turned over page

with unshown modern respect

far away long past prime

and a mind well grounded

down to derelict

seemingly as an open book

with personable people portrayed

they start laughing at all your moves

in a reckoning you can't lament

FORSAKEN OWNED

may I make for myself

a pathway upside down

thinking I care too much of life

when all I want to do is eat

a glutton of the world

soaked up and spread out soul

as pasts tends to fade

futures coming on its own pace

mistakes work for me

possibly in trust never love always

till you've died before you die

these always are fade proof

taken your soul, forsaken my own

pain tapped into the vein

wide open full of moans

flood of anger in my blood

NEXT TO ME

smile at me pretty

let me take you on a walk

to bounce a thought

that has my mind a spin

and you can't tell anyone

or know how it begins

for us two that have no clue

why when life is high

we smile and sigh

because we don't click

with any or the rest of it

while I ponder and delve delusional

overwhelm myself with me

of all this deep dilemma

equal parts apnea and apathy

for the sake of just being near

SOUL GRAVE

my shoulders stay steadfast so belt away

you lippy shit are not worth it

this next life is super

six feet from the top

the belting away won't stop

while sitting in this pit

wallowing in all my shit

I see you up there

standing in my clean air

you are life...and death

a god given body

soul buried and shoddy

alone in a painted silence

wasteful and ready for a colder world

welcoming people to a party

SOCIAL BIRD

pain perches itself

on a high ledge

I cannot reach

it swoops down

to lurk around

in the dark

beside me

I see like a fly

blurred and segmented

but that bird

only sees me

ANXIETY WORLD

minced and crushed herbs

all the garbabbled words

how do I despise myself

how do I disguise myself

pushing in on the pain

painted on again and again

uni-souled world of old

LADY ON THE CLOCK

I press snooze on my muse

cause my head hurts and she gets me

moody too

red light devotion

shadows instilling motion

money from hand to hand

an ancient bought paid brand

war and harmony

nickeled and dimed me

straight up sex crime scream

deceit and lies with troubled eyes

and my fabled fools disguised me

MANIFEST FANTASY

red light monkey

crawls up my back

to sit on my shoulder

and kiss on my neck

this monkey's morals be bought

along a quick wallet check

she scratches, claws, and paws

leaning on my back to soften

her personified object

monkey in a gilded cage

brainwashed honest living wage

old truth never told

part-time pet

empty soul

RELATIONS

gods moving megaliths

like shuffling cards

to stagger stagger fall

stagger walk stagger crawl

always knock things down first

as young people place personalities

upon them

to damn them

CURL UP

going here gone there

balance confronted

in a need of something

wanted

wroughted

to feel molten warm sometimes

I need to feel warm

for warmth

COMPLICATED

I need room to bleed sometimes

just to let my soul take over

to clear a pent-up feeling

free flowing into someone's ear

or on a page

or in silence

smelling what the wind brings

I fall back to let my soul catch me

wrinkly hands strong and compassionate

never seem to drop me

AN ACTOR'S PRETENTIOUS HEART

I slice my veins

so I can bleed my pain

and live life again

on a stage of vain

to walk amongst a crowd

without self-doubt

feeling full and feeling proud

for my name is screamed aloud

FORTUNE #1

direct accomplishments

speaking louder than words

commanding the wisdom of the ages

determining your successes

life as a bold and dashing adventure

stepped on the soil of many countries

you naming yourself

FASHIONABLE DEATH

as she speaks

her pheromones are sweet

contrary to her deceit

but I can see

while she weaves

that golden fleece

to blind me

CORNER COUNTER DELI

titillated tipsy turvy top

just a dumb spun fool

heartwarming and satisfying

to our fresh eyes

caked and coddled

bringing the comforts close

you yourself with one

of these fabulous treats

spoils to any meal

PROPAIN SLAIN

whispers reek of you

a gas line peace pipe

supercharging with time

setting the room alight

whip crackled flames

serpentine curled first strike

soft salt licked wounds

words that sting from spite

strands of spirit echo

burned out and out of sight

whatsoever vigor reigned supreme

integrity feeding frenzied delight

PURGED BLUE BIRD

rattle the love cage

let the little bird fly

lost its song to sing

only emptiness resides

it seeks a new maestro

to strum the strings with pride

writing a new peace of music

replacing the harmony of life

EXPOSED

rage splits my mind

and makes me wander blind

standing in our own shadow

as a man

the loyal glue starts to fail

and shows the pieces of me

cracked concealing a fury

of restrained frenzy fighting

the rule of law

KNIFEWORK

flayed my soul

drained it cold

so I could live a life untold

it didn't get this way on its own

it was coached

my pain has been honed

scratched and picked

cut to the bone

LINES CAN'T TALK

I write so I may

use these pages

as my legs

and the spine

as my own

LIGHTHOUSE

would you like

space from me

miles and miles

across the sea

to only hear me

when the wind whispers

across your ears

let's you smell me

in the salty breeze

that is what the wind

can do for me

and you

of all the loved ones

I wish I could see

FREQUENT FLIGHTS

I have more questions to ask

fully knowing no answer given

would satisfy my anger

the confusions I seem to seek

have peace in solitude

a cool breeze asks nothing of me

no questions of the why

there...only as a friend

a tree in the wind as the song goes

or an unknown creek that slowly flows

befriending another soul

across the plane

with no place to go

no place...or a home

when life seems to wane and fade

PIGEON SOULED

the soul perched on my sleeve

picks up and starts to leave.

big bright red lips

opens its hands and blows

a sent kiss

bon voyage little soul bird...bon voyage

fly away to circle another sky

for another traveler's perch

more deserving than I

TICKET TAKER

two toned tongues

is what they carry

love can be a frivolous thing

as an under-vested life

when 4:50pm is never on-time

while it takes

a winters day patience for

a word

a moment

a rhyme

a life

DESSERT TRAY

if you meet

great unavailable people

that stir you

let them spice your life

let them flavor your soul

a tender tasty treat

full of flavor

and available to eat

a meal for me

a meal for you

feed on a world of people

you don't know

no pressure for prey

only a minds delight

ANALGESIC

is there a game afoot

a dirty job involving soot

the chimney needing a sweep

well I am just that creep

so squeeze me tight

cover all my white

with black dirty shine

that sooty soot left behind

I'LL WALK YOU HOME

you took a bath...drank
then lit a cigarette

a chair in the center of the floor
you were slouched in it

your knees above your waist
and spread out wide

arm dangled between, you blew smoke
out the side of your mouth

as your legs lapsed, you asked
for "just a little mercy"

the jagged words you said
the words I took for apathy

tilted your head back then looked at me
you could do anything

FREE PLATE SOCIETY

write me a future

splendid and true

full of life's colors

except for the blues

a world full of peace

where questions are free

and children can live life

with the wide open eyes

where two faces become one

and as for pain...there is none

COLD SWEATS

a missed chance at melancholy

I dreamt of slander

a mind full of litter

in haste

harsh words explode

and the dirty questions wither

digging deep

only increases the load

on your shoulders

SHADES OF GRACE

weary weathered veins

how many ways to see

the nests of thievery

pushed to the edge

as trust in me

we all must wander together

fateful things failing down

with bruised knees

THINKING OF YOU ALWAYS

leaving orchids

on the front steps

of your own mind

do not know the eyes

having been felt anymore

at the future, by the past

left on that cautious ledge

with only one more breath

left and last

HOW MANY DAYS

hide your assets

in a privacy journal

then disappear

a death package statistic

of vital births

called out in the depths

revolving eternal accounts

WORDS GIVEN

puke on their plate

shoveling it in

feed it all to them

whether they spit it out

the taste always stays

as an idea heir on their tongue

with a dry pallet

and no hunger for me

stuffed full they will say

with never taking a bite

yet still their ears will swallow

all of your words

all of your might

LEAKY WALLET

push me to the edge

and drive me insane

scratching my back

to scream my name

let's play your game

in your head

or on my ledge

drip drop

drip drop

drip

drop

BE VERY QUIET

listening to your peers

joining in their tears

salt lick nipple stains

breast feeding in public causes pain

a snowflake once said

or was that in my head

these days some want to confuse

with an alternate reality

and how you lose

this doesn't rhyme

but don't listen to them

we all grow with time

IT TENDS TO HAUNT ME

got blues on my shoes

no dimes for a shine

sassy little honey

took all my money

a treat treated

as a love slave

the road drove down deep

into the grave

EVERYTHING IN A NAME

specter comes to slit your throat

then changes into a goat

that bucks to cut you

watching you bleed

black blood spews with greed

putting out the flames

AS THE CROWD APPLAUDS

judged by clothes

in famines of grain

a family is hard to lead

stone sharpening blade

absent in a cage

time and circumstance

angry to dull

uneducated they turn into evil

becoming a virtuous fighter of bulls

as the crowd applauds

the barley eater nods

to live another day

CAREER GOALED IN TENSION

orally glorify

with a tainted tongue

whipped and withered

by means and margins

demeanfully gratifying

an existence

BYE GONE ERROR

tales of feeble men

erase the stories

that I try to tell

he who is unique

sees, feels, and tastes

the pain of his life

social abnormalities

introduce an observer

a man amongst a crowd

drawn attention loathed

factors the deciding

of a voice so moved

STARTLED

can I scream tonight

or would tears suffice

the terror rings clear in my ears

and my heart strings are all spliced

pain shall be my binding

the cover all my own

but still confining

LIFE LESSON LEARNED

my core grows cold

sometimes end to end

the scars of an old soul

with dried up tears

on the mend

LITERAL ORATION

a blowjob is worth

one hundred million words

and she spits them all out

as a messy metaphor of cells

in the dirt

and smiles

PARASITIC PROSE

you must boil life

to lick eternity from its sweat

a rust-away wind

smelted as a symphony

tremendous like a swollen shadow

an appetite for what is not said

but bought and paid for

moved

then dead

SWEAT LADEN

live a thick life

as music incubates dreams

floods essential fusions

powering the wicked jest

yields my delicious love

although some will envy

the ecstasy

we leave at that vexed place

SALTY AS THE DAY

scorned by the crowd

for falling down

life has its scrapes and sores

small cuts and abrasions galore

with clumsy simplistic follies

still numb but always jolly

GRAVE GAIT

if you were to walk down a hard line

of wrong or reason

whose path would you follow

or does it sway with the season

a path less traveled

full of many traps and holes

gives way to an unapparelled logic

pondered and good for the soul

prodding along to a similar end

as we all finish the same

life and its selfish meaning

a fucked up ying verses yang

GOLDENFISH

give me a mind

to tilt and whirl

that returns receiving

to an action complete

in a map of mayhem

that bends boundaries

and stretches stability

to the brink

of worthless climaxes

of letting go

of your dizzied selflessness

as our soul's spin

worlds content to collide inside

the clear bowl

LET IT BE

as we call upon it

breathing is a disaster

till we quit

let it be easy

warmth to the touch

comfort in a clutch

room to breathe and move

held tightly to soothe

these things all bleed

allowing life's pain to mend

the only thing on his plate

is a wanderer's fate

breathing is a bomb

which is actually really good

PERIMETER SHRINKAGE

every happy heart

has fell from my shaky hands

so please don't say

I love you

because I have been here longer

than we have

and those words seem to touch

me too deeply

HUMANITARIAN

ladies and gentlemen!

your friend and mine

riding the backdoor pipeline

and what a fine young lady she is too

(round of applause, please.)

CROOKED HALO

a master that starts

to trace the world lines again

will oversee it onto maps

doing things called leading

much like the things doing nothing

and these visionaries who are naughty

could feed love or take it

the malnourished roles

will be played

UGLY GAME OF PRICKS

competitors with generic ideas

have preconsciously thought victories

these veterans have a let down

there is a new way of inquisitive minds

that simply read them

the players around the board

resistance is futile

when we tie the lines

to hook you and watch you dangle

groping your withered wise tongues

and dazzling you with our whit

as you refuse to see that we are aware

you are all just elderly fleas

on the dog of society

feeling as though you have no choice

your eyes covered by a gemmed fleece

you stare in awe at this shiny suit

as it keeps you

SUPER ABSORBENCY

there are those peripheral people

that tend to achieve your dreams

before you do

in their rat race, it is easier

to start from the finish

to improve themselves with a marked start

and marked finish we are then told

they will have performed well

how we apply ourselves in our improvement

determines whether our participation

has even had a value

LATENT LOCKPICK

these peripheral people

and their peripheral visions

deter our children

from birth to rebellion

like everyone else

our humankind's skeletons stay hidden

deep within these

locked limbo look-alike chests

encased in our flesh

the key to this lock box life

is that we all lose on purpose

or have a choice of the unshackled mind

JELLYFISH

my fate

as I come alone

has no words

that are ever said

or ever done

to that breaking point

which is nearly here

as I walk home

no crossing the lines

only this time

the loneliness shows

at a place I almost love

in the drifter's world

which brings

my peace soft and smooth

as it mixes

with all kinds of walks

of life. . . in life

I drift alone

CHEWED SASSY PLASTIC

apologize for the help

cradle the abuse

let them control the ultimatum

there is no guaranteed lifeline

change your level for rank

so the family will burn

on this generation's rollercoaster

beat on them

heal the murder

this life is mine

IMPECUNIOUS EXAMPLE

grimaced old blood

in this homeless man's body

he and his brood morality

have a faithful grave

gravity tugging on his malleable frame

and the preachy ethical lessons

against this so-called freakish beggar

shunning so willingly...sending him quickly

shooing shoeless to anywhere but here

his nowhere...his everywhere place to go

he who bawls, pauses, then abdicates

to himself in concrete cushioned slumber

to stroll along in nomadic fashion

breathing his own absence and deficiency

in existence like us all

one step in front of the other

accepting indirection is not a preference

he is unable to elevate beyond

the bombardment of points and giggles

we should applaud this masterpiece

the human being who survives without

those gaudy illusioned materials of society

they savor in simplicity as we diminish

cherish his character with extravagance

his obscenity needs no pretentious empathy

nor our ego-tripped self-approval masks

however kind unbiased unconditional offerings

endure as much appreciated treasures

in a language you can't understand

verbalizing "bless you" is not for your god

only gratitude in acknowledgement of a human

WHAT SHE DIDN'T LIKE

she never liked to watch me cry

when my eyes would turn blood red

and when the salty droplets tumbled down

my face to fall and stain me

when my glands would swell so it hurt

every time I tried to swallow her

in silence

THOUGHTS ALONG THAT SWIRL

rest peacefully

she'll play notes of love songs

as images constantly held close

by tears running down my face

touching my warm lips

tongue tasting the memories

of voices heard by many years

and a gentle touch once shown

in our pages of time once shared

WAXED PATH

days long in

conceptual beliefs

of death waned pity

have passed

trialing tearful

self-oppressions

unraveling time

with artful attacks

and humanitarianism

practiced upon

everyone close

except yourself

the one deserving

it the most

in an ultimative driven

injustice of life

SINGLE IS SIMPLE

no pleading calls

no days of pity

only patience

which does grow stronger

as is its toll on time

the strong of heart

overcomes the loneliness of life

and death to you

the lonely lonely you

FINGERPRINT

passion burned through

my veins

and tingles the tips

of my fingers

that touched her

MAINSTREAM STITCHING

woven among cavities in the head

beaten black and busted

thousands of the lying dead

they lay there naked

prisoners in a media thread

climate changed full of dread

intertwined creation hollowed out ahead

tied tightly to our earthly bed

simple people cleverly led

social minds all groveling and fed

complex walls of false glory gifted

funneling down in our coward hearth

as a species that is faint of heart

DEAD LIFT DREAM

with the might of a man

who has run

all his life

sometimes I wonder

why

we let the dreams fade

into a heaviness analogous to iron

lifted upon the shoulders

for an insight

as to its reflection

racked upon the mighty

with repetition

ANTIAGING

life lived through hourglassed time

in grains we count each day

no running away

from gravity's slide

patiently waiting out the ending

we stay

drowning in gray grain roots

of wrinkled wrapping

and closing days

across ages overlapping

time always stays

TACTIFIED

I didn't

grow up

with cackles

I never learned

about that hassle

to make people

like me

to like themselves

for which they hate

and that is why

they could never understand

my esteem in me

as a poor being

a pauper king

of dirt and grime

with wealth to give

as a smile with a helping hand

in my crown of humble beginnings

GRIPPED

she holds them down

and strips their body clean

to paralyze them

for a day or two

she likes it low

practically

motionless and teasing

her hunger tears

through their body

scared to be a man

scarring

they watch quivering

at the simple sight

of woman's internal burn

the men strewn along her life

a wake of crispy kindling

and ashes all in petrified piles

SURVIVAL HANDBOOK

getting worked

flustered of the mind

relentless acts of passion

all tied up

limbs fastened tongues twisted

our unveiling

a continual response

to consume

in deadly happy hunger

GLINT

lovely little

laughs

ring about my thoughts

that tickle

my face and bring a smile

OWNED EYES

I saw a woman's eyes today

as she walked by

with a man kissing on her neck

squeezing her hand

feeling along her body

as he gripped tightly

onto her waist

she just looked at me

like she needed to be saved

BDSM BEAUTY

the simple sight

conceals the side of her

that few mortal men

along her life have seen

that naked state

like first arriving in this world

when bearing all her skin

she turns into an animal

throwing humanity completely out

of society's perceived window

a practically unseen masterpiece

she walks the streets

works and eats

like the rest of us

but underneath the human complexion

lurks an animal inside

a way of unmaterialized life

her snarling, while we wait for her

as scared prey waiting on arrival

the lurking parts coming out to devour

ETHEREAL RAMBLING 1

no pleading calls

no crying days of pity

only patience

for love does grow stronger

as patience tends to take

its toll of time

only the strongest of heart

overcome the loneliness of life

without it

ETHEREAL RAMBLING 2

or them

that one person

that can make you laugh

or make you cry

make you hurt

that is the one for your love

it is that person

that gives you those feelings

and emotions

that ache

in the center of your chest

the bottom of your throat

in eyes from which each tear wells

ETHEREAL RAMBLING 3

love

is not a thing of mercy

it is a thing of truth

that sticky

co-dependent

chained too kind

a thing what exists

only to allow

your heart to speak its own

love is better than money

better than sex

better than femininity and manhood alone

love is life

love is freedom

and the passage of all beings

ETHEREAL RAMBLING 4

no day of concept

in belief of death and pity

has thus passed my trial

of years and aggression

having now been given a sight

aimed at practicing appreciation

she was my first love

my true love in heart in mind

with my soul she rests peacefully

as she still plays the notes

of my love songs

ETHEREAL RAMBLING 5

her image constantly

embraced by tears running

dropping down my face

touching my lips

my tongue to taste the memories

seconds spent in a sonnet

oh what tears bring me joy

what tears bring me sorrow

these tears only bring me love

and they will do the same tomorrow

ETHEREAL RAMBLING 6

this comes from my heart

from those feelings

that I have for you

my love if only you

could see my heart

and see my love twisted

though you may not hear its whispers

from miles away

nevertheless they bring weight

by virtue of being said

watch me ache

for your warm embrace

your voice

to be heard by my ears

and the gentle touch

that you once showed me

ETHEREAL RAMBLING 7

this day of reckon

acknowledged pure passion

the page of time

in which you shared with me

has made me a special man

among the thoughts

that swirl about my mind

a conscious thought of me

rather than my disrupted psyche

time

does truly make a love stronger

my time has made me appreciate it

love that is

as awkward as that sounds

TESTING THE ETHER

walks with the breath of your soul

carrying the way of passage

to the world

life generates itself

from lengthy ponderings

grasping images from space

of carved memories

complimentary curved memories

memories kept in mind

for a lifetime of thought

TO CARE FOR ALL

ill-gotten gains

in worlds of sadness

and slow-motion suicides

to be with me

be in mine

in my

distraughtment

distastefully yours

distressedness

as a choice of mine

a gift in the shape

of your liking

the shape of your demise

and mine

just for the act of giving

is an act of living

TSUNAMIED STATE

the ocean

should cover me

so I can scream

with echoes from the deep

that no one hears

because the swells

carry my message away

ONE TIME USE

find concern in release

from a good time

when waterproof people fade

like a day in an emojied sun

with no shade or UV killing rays

some people have a flexible coat

as cold-blooded animals they feed

feasting on all lives indiscreet

the ambush predator bites

but does not eat

they only seek a death roll in sheets

frenzied fucking freebie fully fleshed

just as time expires you're discarded

like a used rubber

unfurled...fully milted...discarded

thrown on the floor for you to clean

promptly swiping right for a new date

with a new match-made they escape

WITH YOU

your eyes speak

a silent scream

that scratches

yells and breathes through you

as loud as church bells

soft as satin

it begins

the race of your heart

a churning stomach

in an intense instant

that reoccurs each time

LONG GONE ECHO

her love was like

walking through sheets

on a clothesline

shadows shining though

silhouettes of her

as permanent as the wind

in my mind

EASY GOING EXIT

don't want to know your name

and wonder of the fit

just want to know your game

and jump right into it

don't need to talk to you

and pretend I care to hear

just want to leave this place aloof

and go away easily unclear

don't need to see you again

and question this anymore

just want to leave this pain

after dropping our clothes on the floor

ANCHORITE SKIN

that person you see in the mirror

breathing from your lungs

within your pores

cradling itself around your bones

structure letting little pieces

dangle through your veins

controlled by your husk of choices

but not you

no never you

INTIMATE INMATE

prisons of wet water-based walls

pulled back

to expose a new opening

of books for the very first time

passages unread

hidden from sight

locked inside these walls

of prismed echoes

and shiny rainbows

so well appropriated

not so well propagated

library of lies

MISHANDLED MESSAGE

hide behind your eyes

and run from me

but I see your soul

as it reaches to breathe

screaming my name

scratching at my brain

in all your silence heard

say not a word

GET BY SOMEDAY

grown on her own

I wish life could be

jazz for her

but not only the notes

should flow

and roam

aloud

but the tone of freedom

a no malice harmony

composed

but has yet to be played

in a symphony sung alone

ONE SOUL WON

if a spirit intertwines itself

they must be the one

to tame demons you harbor

and quell the damage you've done

trying to unravel the many years

where you have slowly become

a shadow undone with prizes won

IN CHORUS

lower your life

and come back into it

washing in a sync of sorrows

give yourself room for movement

to soak up the shit and slop

with an atrocious empathy mop

to be rung out and rang aloud

as though everything is the same

when the untamed is suggested harmless

we are all insane

so let your soul breathe

as the wind or we won't see each other

only the lovely little lies

we sing together

TAILORED WOUND

as empty as my pockets
my hands hold
what you cannot see
a wind again in my weathered veins
never staying too long to grieve

as a breeze, as a moment
hands in time that held
like gloves tapered to your fingers

it can never stay on too long
as it is too warm
when it turns to love
frigidness is comfortable
because it is so well known

seemingly fine fitting and worn
broken in with creases
scuffs and wear marks
only my hands could make

I will remember you without regret

for never staying too long

there are no excuses

only choices in a chosen fate

hard to regret what you don't loose

it is love who knows it won't

grit and grime of work well done

wind weathered in oiled leather

these gloves are now your own

but still blisters bleeding now healing

go alone into the mist

naked and cold

with pockets as empty as my own

GRIMEY RHYME

life including some confusion

sex with a little delusion

nice and clean and sometimes gaudy

not with mind, but definitely body

not what is said and should

unclearly stated how it stood

feeling the compassion

for a little black book of ration

the untrue and tall tails

of their friend that scratches with her nails

kissing this human trough

makes ponderings of blowing them off

thinking in the long run

what is to be done

when sexual pleasures are free

with no kind of daily fee

why should you change

this complete derange

more meaning is favored and wanted

not what has been so well flaunted

needing that intimate and romantic touch

not jumping in with that right now clutch

although the rough stuff is fine and well

when all the time, it ceases to sell

giving it all a little more time

makes everything sorta rhyme

knowing which path is your way

can determine whether you will or won't stay

leaving them is probably the best choice

but be sure to listen to your inner-voice

to the thinking you must do

only the decision can be made by you

it's not your friend's or family's affair

just whether you do or don't care

never a decision completely just

through love and life we do what we must

could it be different for you

it felt good to me too

the misleading and mischievous fact

or and honest and true act

who knows what to believe

finish it and just leave

The final pages are Existential Abstractions... these are some simple words to describe an essence or give small fragments of each poem.

Kernels of an image if you are lost by my intention...or sometimes to enable an abstract place to get lost in thought.

Completely your own interpretation though, these riddles and rambles have no sacred answers.

Ultimately if you find yourself going back time and time again to seek an understanding or find the usefulness in a metaphor, then maybe I've done a good job.

It's all about seeking connection...or creating them. Thank You.

EXISTENTIAL ABSTRACTIONS

13 please promise a lie || future / life / speculation

14 open || unconditional love / giving / downtrodden

15 which is what I need || life / future / love / giving / information

16 religious death || religion / idea / existence / death

17 murder matrimony || family / death / betray

18 family dementia || obsolete / age / misleading care

19 forsaken word || sex / drugs / future / past / relationships

20 next to me || love / wrong / proposal

21 soul grave || death / buried / self-esteem / depression

22 social bird || logic / vision / reflection / torment

23 anxiety world || disguised / worry / reflection

24 lady on the clock || prostitution / lust / sex

25 manifest fantasy || prostitution / soul / perspective

26 relations || youth / canceling / blaming / discourse

27 curl up || loss / warmth / connection

28 complicated || soul / art / compassion

29 an actor's pretentious heart || pain / soul / pride / actor

30 fortune #1 || travel / choice / explorer

31 fashionable death || lust / love / betray

32 corner counter deli || prostitution / gluttonous / advertising

33 propain slain || anger / relationships / sneaky / bi-polar

34 purged blue bird || lost love / heart / harmony

35 exposed || manhood / abrasive / tenacious / truth to power

36 knifework || pain / soul / life / division

37 lines can't talk || courage / determination / strength

38 lighthouse || love / longing / time

39 frequent flights || anger / travel / time

40 pigeon souled || love / introvert / speculative

41 ticket taker || relationships / time / lies

42 dessert tray || friends / conversation / soul

43 analgesic || playing games / sex / lust / dirty job

44 i'll walk you home || sex / lust / love / hate / remorse

45 free plate society || future / peace / pain

46 cold sweats || melancholy / concern / smear

47 shades of grace || integrity / life / time

48 thinking of you always || death / solitude / in-mind / loss

49 how many days || secrecy / truths / hide / inheritance

50 words given || communication / understanding / empty

51 leaky wallet || sex / addiction / gambling / prostitution

52 be very quiet || overstep / not listening / no conversation

53 it tends to haunt me || gold-digger / sex / money / opportunity

54 everything in a name || greed / anger / ghosts / dreaming

55 as the crowd applauds || judgement / time / poverty / killing

56 career goaled in tension || life / self-worth / opportunity manipulation

57 bye gone error || understanding / poet / history / vigilant

58 startled || dreams / hidden / pain

59 life lesson learned || scars / soul / healing

60 literal oration || not listening / procreation / sex / dishonest

61 parasitic prose || cleansing / capitalism / death

62 sweat laden || sex / love / intensity / life / captivation

63 salty as the day || embarrassed / strong / vulnerable

64 grave gait || self-reliant / thought tinkerer / agency

65 goldenfish || ideas / pathways / debate / climate / discourse

66 let it be || life / perspective / release / anger

67 perimeter shrinkage || love lost / longing / solitude

68 humanitarian || fetish / sex / appreciation

69 crooked halo || social / roles to play / individual / power

70 ugly game of pricks || change / individuality / sincerity / meekness

72 super absorbency || social / privilege / perspective

73 latent lockpick || social / oppression / choice

74 jellyfish || thought / experiences / learning / myself / nomadic

75 chewed sassy plastic || strength of mind / oppression / direction / life

76 impecunious example || homelessness / undervalued / understanding

78 what she didn't like || vulnerable / crying / silence

79 thoughts along that swirl || vulnerability / memories / mixed relationship

80 waxed path || acceptance / self-oppression / self-esteem

81 single is simple || lonely / alone / death / excluded